Psalms From The Pathway

Musings of an ordinary pilgrim
upon the Extraordinary

by

Lois Williams

xulon
PRESS

Xulon Press
www.XulonPress.com

Xulon Press books are available in bookstores everywhere,
and on the Web at www.XulonPress.com..

Dedication

The thoughts in this book are dedicated
to my Heavenly Father
from Whom they were received,
and to Whom
all the glory belongs.

Contents

Acknowledgments

There are so many people to thank for their help and support I could not name them all. My family and friends, pastors and teachers, I praise God for you. There are a few, however, whom I want to mention specifically.

First, Patricia Roberts, who kick-started a long-buried dream by saying "Why don't you write it yourself?", then followed that suggestion with years of encouragement. I thank you.

My friend Sharon Goddard, whose ears were almost always the first to hear the words as they rolled from my heart through my computer, and who has wept with me and cheered for me as I crawled, walked, and sometimes ran, along my pathway. I cherish you.

Paulette Buskirk, whose wise counsel and depth of understanding have been a source of accountability, and whose tears of shared emotion have brought me over and over again to the throne of God in worship. I am grateful for you.

And there's the Thursday morning coffee group. This miniature church filled with godly women has, individually and corporately, loved and affirmed me, supported and cared for me, laughed and prayed with me and shown me the beauty of the body of Christ when it really works! I appreciate you all.

Last, my husband Fred. It's difficult to express the depth of my gratitude to God for giving me this man to share my life. Working with the Master Architect, his steadfast faith and solid strength have built a foundation for me, and his love, the most unconditional I have ever experienced in human form, has given me a building permit. I love you with all my heart.

Psalms from the Pathway

Foreword

Keeping a spiritual journal is a tool God is using in my life to draw me to Him. It is through reflecting upon His Word and its application in my life that healing water pours upon my soul. For most of my life there was a rebellious and angry spirit within me that prevented any real communion with God. A few short years ago I finally heard His call on my life, accepted His forgiveness and began to experience the joy that accompanies surrender. And I began sharing with friends the words that poured from my heart. What I was hearing from Him and writing to Him was finding a resonance in the lives of others.

Though *Psalms From The Pathway* is a very personal book, I trust that those who share the pathway with me will find refreshment for the journey and an anticipation of each new step.

It is with gratitude to my heavenly Father that I offer these devotional meditations, whispered into the heart of an ordinary person, who seeks only to know the Extraordinary God and to make Him known.

"Return to Me,
for I have redeemed you."
Isaiah 44:22 (NIV)

INVITATION

"This is what the LORD says: 'Stand at the crossroads and look; ask for the ancient paths, ask where the good way is, and walk in it, and you will find rest for your souls.'"
Jeremiah 6:16 (NIV)

I seem to be standing
immobile
at a crossroad,
yearning to know the peace
of the center of God's will.
My heart is crying,
pleading for His direction.
Surely He will show me
where He wants me,
so I listen,
careful to discern His presence,
hear the whisper in my soul.
Then He speaks
and in the very depths of me
I sense His arms outstretched
in welcome.
His guiding voice,
so tender, breathes,
"Come here."

HANDCRAFTED

*"But now thus saith the LORD that created thee, O Jacob,
and he that formed thee, O Israel, 'Fear not; for I have
redeemed thee, I have called thee by thy name; thou art
mine." Isaiah 43:1*

He formed me.
God took His thought
that carried my name
and with hands tender and firm
squeezed my formlessness
through His fingers,
shaping, molding,
building a person
crafted by His touch,
unique.

He made me.
God took my days, and
determining their frame and texture,
set them in motion with the breath
that fills with life.
He placed me here,
birthed into a fallen world,
then gently began
calling my name.

DEEP STILLNESS

"Deep calls to deep at the roar of your waterfalls; all your waves and breakers have swept over me." Psalm 42:7 (NIV)

Tramping through my thoughts
as though hiking in the woods,
I happen across an inviting pond.
Clear, calm, deep, it beckons my soul.
Sensing its pull in the center of my being
I long to slip into its cool depths.
It is the very heart of God seeking me,
drawing me into poignant communion.

Yet were I to plunge in,
encumbered as I am
with earthly trappings,
I would be unable to stay afloat.
To be caressed by the silken
waters of the pond I cannot dive in
and simply splash across its surface.
To be immersed
in the stillness of His Spirit,
I must be stripped
of self-righteous garments,
pride and incessant striving.
The depths of my heart answer
the call of Your deep stillness, oh God.
I will submit, and rest
in the buoyancy of Your love
that wraps and cleanses
and renews my soul.

SHORELINE

"Blessed be the LORD, who daily loadeth us with benefits, even the God of our salvation." Psalm 68:19

How can I explain this
tugging at my heart,
the desire for God that
I am experiencing?
I walk along the shoreline,
mesmerized by the water's
incessant movement,
rolling out and rushing back.
The water can no more resist
the heavenly pull than I can resist
the longing I feel.

And so I am thinking,
in much the same way,
God calls my heart to Himself.
When my spirit rolls toward Him
in response,
He reminds me that there is more.
He is not finished,
and rushing back
with inevitable blessings,
as the frothy bubbles
slide back upon the sand,
He floods the shoreline
of my soul.

ANTICIPATION

"Since ancient times no one has heard, no ear has perceived, no eye has seen any God besides you, who acts on behalf of those who wait for him." Isaiah 64:4 (NIV)

The walk back home from the mailbox
is dreary when there are no letters,
only bills and solicitations.
And entering the house
with no flashing light
on the answering machine
makes me a little lonely sometimes.

How anxious I am to hear
from my family...children far away,
brothers and sisters,
distanced by miles, divergent lives.
My life is busy, too, and many times
I fail to keep in touch with those I love.
I'm not attaching blame,
just longing to hear.

So when I rest with open Bible,
head bowed to pray,
my heart hears,
and understands,
His welcome,
"I've been waiting to hear from you."

HEART'S DESIRE

"One thing have I desired of the LORD, that will I seek after; that I may dwell in the house of the LORD all the days of my life, to behold the beauty of the LORD, and to enquire in His temple." Psalm 27:4

Small arms wrapped around my neck,
snuggling into my lap, she announced,
"Grandma, I'm finally here.
I can hug you all I want,
and that's all I came for."

Though swelled with joy,
my heart nearly broke,
for deep in my soul
I saw my approach to my Heavenly Father.
His joy when I come to Him
surely is quelled when I simply
haul out my shopping list.
Does He ever hear from me
those tender words?

Father, teach me to snuggle into Your lap
and whisper, "Here I am.
Let me hug You.
My heart's desire
is to feel Your nearness…
and that's all I came for."

THE DAM

"For I am persuaded that neither death, nor life, nor angels, nor principalities, nor powers, nor things present, nor things to come, nor height, nor depth, nor any other creature, shall be able to separate us from the love of God which is in Christ Jesus our Lord." Romans 8:38-39

Your love is a mighty river,
oh God,
rushing, bubbling, tumbling,
never still,
always moving toward me.

I think, though,
I've blocked the power of Your love
by damming the river
with a barrier of stubbornness
to have my own way.

Yes, a trickle comes through,
but a lake of love waits to breach the dam
and flood the valley.
Help me, Father,
to smash the dam
in unreserved surrender.

Have Your own way.

THE CORE

"Be still and know that I am God." Psalm 46:10

It is intimacy that I desire,
connection,
communication,
commitment,
at the core of my being.

Simplicity is vital for
communion to occur.
Life must move around the stillness,
for quietness is difficult to carve
from noise and busyness.

In an apple,
the essence rests in the core
and sweet tasty fruit
grows from the center.
In the same way,
from solitude's essence
comes intimacy,
and fruit is the result.
Without a quiet place at the core,
life is stunted, barren,
spinning uselessly.

Yes, it is intimacy that I desire
at the very core of my being.

THE SECRET PLACE

"He that dwelleth in the secret place of the Most High shall abide under the shadow of the Almighty." Psalm 91:1

Where is Your secret place, dear God?
I yearn to go there to dwell,
to rest beneath Your wings.
Only in that secret place is the certainty
of Your promise of protection,
oh Most High.

I search the pages of Your book and learn
that Moses asked, like me,
to discover You in intimacy.
You cleaved a rock, hid him there,
and Your glory passed close by.

My search leads to another Rock,
this One cleft for me upon a cross,
breast torn, the heart of God revealed.
In Christ I find the secret place
where I must dwell, and He in me
under the shadow of the Almighty.

REST

" 'If you keep your feet from breaking the Sabbath and from doing as you please on my holy day, if you call the Sabbath a delight and the Lord's holy day honorable, and if you honor it by not going your own way and not doing as you please or speaking idle words, then you will find your joy in the Lord and I will cause you to ride on the heights of the land and to feast on the inheritance of your father Jacob.' The mouth of the Lord has spoken." Isaiah 58:13-14 (NIV)

Somewhere in the Sabbath pause
there waits a place of rest...
the center of my soul.
Where noise recedes, the clamoring ceases
and God's whisper is the only sound
my heart resolves to hear.

A sweet and tranquil breathing space
amid the tasks of life...
the center of my soul.
Where His word is food
and prayer is drink,
where I absorb His essence
to refresh and nurture me.
God designed the Sabbath rest,
fashioned it to meet me there...
in the center of my soul.
Thus, life can swirl around that place
where intimacy has control
and peace flows out in healing waves
from the center of my soul.

CLINGING ARMS

"That ye put off concerning the former conversation the old man, which is corrupt according to the deceitful lusts; and be renewed in the spirit of your mind; and that ye put on the new man, which after God is created in righteousness and true holiness." Ephesians 4:22-24

An embrace embodies affection,
longing, yearning,
an expressive desire to hold closely
a loved one, an idea, a belief.
How often my words shout
a need for intimacy
yet, ignoring the outstretched arms
of my Savior,
my arms stubbornly continue
their earthbound clinging.
I long for revival, renewal,
but I just realized, new life has no room
to grow in a soul whose arms
are wrapped around this world.
Asking for your embrace, Lord,
demands my own limbs outstretched,
free to receive,
to enfold and be enfolded in
your clinging arms.

ENSNARED

"Come unto Me, all ye that labor and are heavy laden, and I will give you rest. Take my yoke upon you, and learn of me, for I am meek and lowly in heart, and ye shall find rest unto your souls. For my yoke is easy and my burden is light." Matthew 11:28-30

"Too busy."
It's my anguished cry.
Too busy to pray,
too busy to spend a quiet hour with God,
too frantic to hear Him,
too important to embrace Him.
There are things I must do.

Have I fallen into the service trap?
More and more I am ensnared,
and sense the trap snapping shut.
I'm unable to pull out of it for
fear of cutting off my leg.
I wonder, though, isn't a crippled leg
more desirable than a frenetic, useless life?
The more I struggle, the tighter
the trap closes and I long for release.
Please, God, if I jerk myself free,
no matter what the pain,
is there room on your lap
for another wounded lamb?

BREAKING THE FAST

*"And as he, (Elijah) lay and slept under a juniper tree,
behold, then an angel touched him, and said unto him,
'Arise and eat'. And he looked and behold there was a
cake baked on the coals, and a cruse of water at his head.
And he did eat and drink." 1 Kings 19:5, 6*

Breakfast is ready.
The table is set,
the food prepared.
"Come, eat", says the Father.
He seats Himself at the head of the table
and waits for us to join Him.
He has come as far as He will,
and we can't taste the richness
of the feast until we pull
our chairs up to the table,
pick up a fork and say,
"I *will* eat. Please pass the food."

So many times we hear the invitation,
smell the delicious aroma
and feel the rumble of hunger,
only to back away and mutter,
"Breakfast will have to wait.
I am too busy."
God won't force feed us.
We must want to eat; desire His food
so much that nothing else matters.
The door of the dining hall is open;
all is ready. Are you hungry?
I accepted His invitation
to breakfast today.
My soul is satisfied.

REDEMPTION

"Jesus, when He had cried again with a loud voice, yielded up the ghost. And behold, the veil of the temple was rent in twain from the top to the bottom; and the earth did quake, and the rocks rent." Matthew 27:50-51

A cross punctures
the mournful sky;
tears of heaven
fall.

Earth's full hope
thrusts with that cross,
and rests in Christ
who gave
His all.

ABANDON

"Then Peter said to him, "Lo, we have left all and followed thee." Luke18:28

Like a shell
lying on the beach,
life removed,
dead,
cast off like armor
after the battle is over,
I leave the husk of self behind,
freely offering the tenderness
of my brand new heart
to the cradling of
my Father's arms.

"He that hath the Son hath life; and he that hath not the Son of God hath not life." 1 John 5:12

Get wisdom, get understanding; do not forget my
words or swerve from them.
Proverbs 4:5 (NIV)

DIGGING

*"How sweet are thy words unto my taste! Yea, sweeter
than honey to my mouth." Psalm 119:103*

Often when I open my Bible
and sense the enormity of its message,
I am staggered at the
truths I want to pursue.
But I sit and wonder where to begin,
it is so full, so rich.
And I guess it's rather like dessert
to a chocolate lover, it must be eaten,
absorbed spoonful by spoonful.

There's no benefit in using a spade;
one cannot consume
a shovelful in a sitting.
But teaspoon by teaspoon,
digging can begin.

NAKED HEART

*"I know that nothing good lives in me, that is, in my sinful
nature. For I have the desire to do what is good, but I
cannot carry it out." Romans 7:18 (NIV)*

I have always dressed my heart
in lovely, caring deeds,
preening its appearance
to be pleasing to my God.
Evil lurking there
was not something I cared to consider;
it would not be acceptable.
A dream wakened me, though, last night,
full of violence and corrupt thought.
Such desecrating impurity, from where?

From my heart, my naked heart,
undressed now of its pious works.
Shivering at the sight of my sin,
I am finally aware that
in my flesh dwells no good thing.
That is why, this morning,
in abject repentance I stand,
sensing at last with my spirit
the power of the miracle,
that Christ drapes my naked heart
with His robe of righteousness
and presents me
spotless before my Maker.
My heart is clothed.

LOVE LANGUAGE

"For the ear trieth words as the mouth tasteth meat."
Job 34:3

"The words that I speak unto you, they are spirit, and they
are life." John 6:63

I love words,
especially words of praise.
It has become vital to me to hear them.
I hunger for words of love and approval,
and so I look for them,
the words that are my love language,
seeking and savoring them,
relying upon them.
I know it is disobedience.

Just the other day, though,
as I was again asking for forgiveness
for this transgression in my life,
God murmured, "Have you considered
all the words I have prepared for you?
I gave you a whole book of words."
Words that tell you of your worth to Me.

I am humbled.
Why do I need words from people
when the Word Himself wrote His
love for me on a cross?
His love language
resounds in my heart.

NECESSARY FOOD

"Neither have I gone back from the commandment of His lips; I have esteemed the words of His mouth more than my necessary food." Job 23:12

The merest exhalation of God
is able to breathe a soul into man,
to infuse the minds in days of old
with holy Scripture.

Last night His breath
brushed my cheek
when once again my heart heard
precious words spoken anew.

The same power that
breathed my soul into me
breathed the words
which feed that soul.

Your Word, O Lord,
is my necessary food.

SOUL OASIS

"For I will pour water upon him that is thirsty, and floods
upon the dry ground: I will pour my spirit upon thy seed,
and my blessing upon thine offspring; and they shall spring
up as among the grass, as willows by the water courses."
Isaiah 44:3, 4

Often as I plod along in my daily walk
I fail to acknowledge my thirst for God.
Busy with my appointed tasks,
I think I will get a drink of living water
in a few minutes.
Minutes turn into hours, and hours into days
until the oasis beckons with its verdant beauty
and my tongue, thick with thirst,
croaks a dusty whisper,
"Just a sip, just a sip of relief…"

But how generous is my God!
Instead of a sip, He pours water upon me.
He cures the dangerous spiritual dehydration,
not with drips but with bucketfuls.

Lord, I want to gulp the living water
of Your word, let it soak into the depths
of my soul lest I dry up into chaff
that the wind can blow away.
Keep me camped beside the oasis,
for in wandering the desert I may survive,
but surely never will I thrive.

FOUNTAIN IN THE VALLEY

*"When the poor and needy seek water, and there is none,
and their tongue faileth for thirst, I the LORD will hear
them, I the God of Israel will not forsake them. I will open
rivers in high places, and fountains in the midst of the
valleys; I will make the wilderness a pool of water, and the
dry land springs of water." Isaiah 41:17-18*

I stumble into the valley,
soul-dry, thirsty,
choking on dust kicked up
by rebellious heels,
my spirit a desert.

Mountain-top euphoria
is a distant memory
to which I long to return,
but strength is needed for the climb
and I am dry.

Where is the delight? The joy?
Eclipsed by selfish goals
I turned my face from Yours
and I am dry.

Here in the valley a fountain waits,
a waterspout for my parched heart.
A pool in the wilderness to quench and cool.
The pages of Your Word
are life-giving rivers.
I drink, and am no longer dry.

SATISFACTION

"O satisfy us early with thy mercy; that we may rejoice and be glad all our days." Psalm 90:14

Satisfaction.
Nothing more required, or desired.
Yet even as I say "I am satisfied,"
my eyes cast about for the next acquisition,
the next project, the next goal.
Satisfied, or temporarily mollified?

Satisfaction speaks of the quenched yearning
which everyone seeks, and though
it cannot be an actuality in the temporal,
spiritually it is completeness
we find only in Christ.

Pure gratitude simply says "Thank You",
resting in sufficiency, undemanding,
not desiring more.
God was satisfied
by the sacrifice of His Son;
nothing else was,
nor ever will be,
required or desired.

May I learn to live in
satisfaction.

SUFFICIENCY

"For He satisfieth the longing soul, and filleth the hungry soul with goodness." Psalm 107:9

For longings deep within our hearts
He comes to bring sweet ease.
The hunger we seek to satisfy
in Him alone can find relief.

We celebrate His coming
with joy and gratitude
but instead of taking all He offers
we leave the manger, hearts unfilled and,
empty,
wander back to lives
consumed with hunger.

He comes, the Prince of Peace.
He gives, Himself the Gift.
He satisfies, completely.
It is good to taste and see that the
Lord is sufficient to bring completeness
to the one who trusts in Him.

BROKEN CISTERN

"For my people have committed two evils; they have forsaken me, the fountain of living waters, and hewed them out cisterns, broken cisterns, that can hold no water."
Jeremiah 2:13

Forsaking You, God,
the fountain of living waters,
I have dug a broken cistern,
a leaky well filled over and over again
with my good deeds,
yet find it continually empty.
I did not realize that in the digging
it was You I was forsaking.

God, please plug up that broken cistern,
my disobedient creation,
as I run into Your arms, returning.
And fill me from the fountain of You
so I overflow with Your love, Your life,
instead of simply leaking
the feeble efforts
of my own making.

FORGIVENESS

"I will sprinkle clean water upon you, and you shall be clean; I will cleanse you from all your impurities and from all your idols." Ezekiel 36:25 (NIV)

Confession, forgiveness, cleansing,
how precious God's promise!
It reminds me of the days in the past
when doing laundry depended
on sunny days, and effort.
The memory, though, also brings
the lovely scent of clean white sheets
damp from the washing machine
stretched out on the clothesline
to receive the drying sun.

And so I was thinking what complete joy
there is in being forgiven, white and clean.
The pure water, purchased by Christ's blood,
sparkling like morning dew
on my white-robed heart.
May my life always be like the
fragrant, damp sheets
hung on the clothesline,
freshly sprinkled with God's forgiveness,
stretched out to receive
the warmth and light of His Son.

THE HEALING

"How good it is to sing praises to our God, how pleasant and fitting to praise him! He heals the brokenhearted and binds up their wounds." Psalm 147:1(NIV)

"He himself bore our sins in his body on the tree, so that we might die to sins and live for righteousness; by his wounds you have been healed." 1 Peter 2:24 (NIV)

I bring my wounded soul,
broken, sore and bleeding,
to You, the one whose written word
promises my healing.
I have been here before,
my cuts were stitched, salve applied,
but I disobeyed and loosed the scab,
sin tore it open wide.

O, Great Physician, here I stand,
my contrite heart revealing need
of soothing balm, your holy word.
As Your forgiveness cleans the gash,
tender skin begins to grow
and mending starts anew.
I claim Your healing now,
but my mind becomes aware,
it's more a process than a one-time deed
and I will fall, unclose the wound,
again to hurt and bleed.

Yet every time you touch the pain,
cleanse the festering scar,
it heals a little more.
One day it will only be a mark
to remind me of the wounds
You'll carry in Your flesh eternally.
By those stripes I am healed.

SHELTER

"For you have been my refuge, a strong tower against the foe. I long to dwell in your tent forever and take refuge in the shelter of your wings." Psalm 61:3-4

Just the other day I was thinking,
in the middle of a windstorm,
how grateful I am for shelter.
A beautiful word, shelter,
and all that it represents.
Such a basic need, sought when one is
threatened, frightened,
cold, hungry, lonely, lost.
And I began to thank God
for all the shelter
He provides me.

First of all, His love covers me.
I am safe with Him.
My husband's love is a refuge
for my heart.
I am safe there, too.
My home, warm and dry,
and filled with comforts,
is a sanctuary for my physical being.

But if all my comfort disappeared
I would still have the
greatest shelter He's provided,
the shelter of salvation
that protects my eternity.

ON THE HEELS OF THE STORM

*"He giveth snow like wool; he scattereth the hoarfrost like
ashes. He casteth forth his ice like morsels; who can stand
before his cold? He sendeth out his word, and melteth
them; he causeth his wind to blow, and the waters flow.
Praise ye the LORD. Praise ye the LORD from the
heavens; praise him in the heights." Psalm 147:17-18,
148:1*

Snowbound, housebound, by the storm
I sit by the window contemplating
the distortion it has created.
Evergreens, shrubs and ferns
are shrouded in white,
their branches bowed low
beneath the weight of the snow.
All is silent, hushed under
a canopy of gray-white sky.

Then through a gap in the frosty boughs
a gleam of light appears
and the sun breaks out,
transforming the overhead to blue.
Experience tells me that soon
the snow will melt from its warmth
and the laden branches will slowly lift
with the disappearing burden.
Familiar shapes will return.

Sometimes I am bent low beneath
the burden left by a storm in my life.
There is no color in
the periphery of my vision.
I must remember that the Son of God
longs to break forth in my heart.
Experience tells me His presence
will melt the cares and
bring sparkle and clarity,
and lift my arms in praise.

Maybe I can only see a gleam of Him
through the shrouded trees of my pain,
but it is enough…for now.

THE PRESENT

*"As God's fellow workers we urge you not to receive God's
grace in vain. For he says 'In the time of my favor I heard
you, and in the day of salvation I helped you.' I tell you now
is the time of God's favor, now is the day of salvation"
2 Corinthians 6:1, 2 (NIV)*

Grace.
It used to be easy to define
when I didn't understand it.
In newness of discovery
the reality of grace is like
a present I've just unwrapped.
Peering inside,
I am amazed that someone
would give me such a marvelous gift,
but to experience it fully
it must be removed from the box.
I examine it as though it were a new garment,
aware somehow it will be a good fit,
because the One Who gave it
knows me well.
But how will it look on me?
And how will wearing it affect my life?
Trembling with anticipation
I clutch it tightly
and head for the dressing room.

ANTITHESIS

"...as sorrowful, yet always rejoicing; as poor, yet making many rich; as having nothing, and yet possessing all things." 2 Corinthians 6:10

I am of the wealthy poor,
riches unseen by human eyes.
Around me stream
the poverty-stricken wealthy,
proudly preening goods, success.
Empty-eyed, frantic,
they search for one more dollar,
one more accolade.

I was once poor as they,
until I struck the gold of eternal wealth.
The affluence of my soul is felt deeply,
and my heart abounds
in the luxury of love
that must be wisely spent .

The penury of this world,
swathed in fragile,
vain veils of opulence,
needs so desperately to mine
the vein of gold that awaits
at the foot of the cross,
exchanging possessions
for possession of treasure untold.

PAID IN FULL

"And by that will, we have been made holy through the
sacrifice of the body of Jesus Christ once for all, because
by one sacrifice he has made perfect forever those who are
being made holy." Hebrews 10:10, 12 (NIV)

Writing checks to pay the bills
the other day I was musing,
wondering how it would be if I
didn't have to pay any bills;
if everything was paid for and
there would be no more little
window envelopes filling the mailbox.

Something I had read recently
about managing debt came to mind,
advice given to struggling individuals:
Refinance, consolidate,
borrow creatively and,
failing all else, seek help.
But none of these takes away the debt,
it only changes the creditor.

My thoughts turned to
the debt of sin we owe.
Man tries all sorts of ways to bargain,
to brush away the phantom,
yet the debt never goes away
until all else fails and he seeks help,
and Discovers, that,
should we choose to accept it,
the Master in Charge has given us
a Visa for heaven, paid in full!

WAGES

"...and when she could no longer hide him, she took for him an ark of bulrushes, and daubed it with slime and with pitch, and put the child therein; and she laid it in the flags by the river's brink ...and the maid went and called the child's mother. And Pharoah's daughter said unto her, 'Take this child away, and nurse it for me and I will give thee thy wages.'" Exodus 2:3, 8-9

Receiving wages for doing
what the heart longs to do,
the ultimate in soul satisfaction.

I was thinking of Moses' mother
setting her baby adrift with nothing but hope.
How anguished her heart must have been as
she turned him loose!
And then, to be brought
to Pharoah's daughter
and promised wages
to do exactly as
her exultant heart yearned!

Sometimes our wages cannot
be placed in the bank.
The reward of having done
what God desires is simply having done it.
Blending the heart of God
with the longing He places in us
and carrying out His plan
pay wages that fill
the pockets of our souls.

THE SHEPHERD'S SHOULDERS

"What man of you, having an hundred sheep, if he lose one of them, doth not leave the ninety and nine in the wilderness, and go after that which was lost, until he find it? And when he hath found it, he layeth it on his shoulders, rejoicing." Luke 15:3-5

There is, in Scripture,
a story from Jesus' lips
about a sheep, lost.
Out of the flock of one hundred,
one, and only one, was missing.

The burden of His wandering sheep
lies heavy on the Shepherd's shoulders.
Shoulders that bore lash marks for His sheep,
shoulders that sagged upon a cross
under the weight of sin.

It was me, that lost sheep,
wandering away, willfully leaving
the Shepherd's arms,
caught in the brambles
far from the sheepfold.
I know it was for me
the Shepherd came looking,
and hearing my bleats of distress,
He found me, laid me across
those mighty shoulders and
joyfully carried me home.

WHAT ABOUT ISAAC?

"And Abraham stretched forth his hand, and took the knife
to slay his son. And the angel of the LORD called unto him
out of heaven, and said, 'Abraham, Abraham', and he said,
'Here am I'. And he said 'Lay not thine hand upon the
lad, neither do thou any thing unto him; for now I know
that thou fearest God, seeing thou has not withheld thy son,
thine only son, from me." Genesis 22:10-12

Faith in the life of Abraham
is played out in obedience.
Praised for generations for his willingness
to sacrifice the one he loved,
he is known for an act that to me
seems almost unbelievable.

But what about Isaac,
lying on the altar, his life threatened?
Did he struggle against the ropes,
or did he simply acquiesce to his father's will?
Scripture is silent; the scene picturing
the obedient Son of God nailed
to a cross, the eternal sacrifice.

So I marvel at Isaac,
his questions answered
with a promise of God's provision,
trusting in his father's love.

And what about me? Is my faith
strong enough to obey God's voice
when He asks me to sacrifice my self,
my pride, my desires, my will?
I want to offer my life upon His altar,

bound by ropes of trust in His love,
positioned for service,
provisioned by His spirit,
abandoned to His will.

Just like Isaac.

UNDERBRUSH

*"Be not conformed to this world, but ye transformed by the
renewing of your mind, that ye may prove what is that
good, and acceptable, and perfect, will of God."*
Romans 12:2

Walking in autumn along the road
I am gazing at the underbrush and,
looking into my life,
seeing a parallel somehow.
A new layer of dead leaves
covers budding growth,
much as the stratum of disobedience
I am struggling with today threatens
to smother my faith,
and the jungle of my tangled past
strives to entwine my roots.

But then I look up.

From tangled underbrush, twisted and dry,
to trees standing tall against the sky,
understanding that the leafy mulch
and withered branches return to dust
to be absorbed, nurturing the soil.
So it is within my soul.
God says He will take away
the former things
if I will keep my eyes on Him,
and from the snarl of sin and shame
He'll straighten, nurture, rearrange,
and raise me up to praise His name.

GLORY

" 'But let him that glorieth glory in this, that he
understandeth and knoweth Me, that I am the LORD which
exercise lovingkindness, judgment and righteousness, in the
earth; for in these things I delight,' saith the LORD."
Jeremiah 9:24

I saw a celebrity the other day,
up close and personal, as they say.
Elbowed and jostled my way up front
in hopes I'd be noticed for a moment,
and then I could say in a casual way,
"Guess who I met the other day?"
With name-dropping aplomb,
I'd bask in the glory surrounding the star.

But I already know the Greatest,
the Celebrity of all time.
I need not jostle nor elbow to get close.
He's always by my side.
The Creator of the stars (celebrities, too)
waits for me to drop His name,
yearns that I pursue those things
that delight Him,
living in such a way that I reflect
His glory.

I WONDER...

"And Jesus cried with a loud voice, and gave up the ghost,
and the veil of the temple was rent in twain from the top to
the bottom. And when the centurion, which stood over
against him, saw that he so cried out, and gave up the
ghost, he said, 'Truly this man was the Son of God.'"
Mark 15:38, 39

I wonder...
about the priests in the temple that day
(the day the veil was torn).
Did they rush headlong
into the Holy of Holies
which had so long been forbidden?

I wonder...
as noon-time darkness
enveloped the temple and quaking
tossed them to the ground,
did they peer fearfully inside
at sights they'd never seen before?

I wonder...
was the light in the lampstand extinguished
with the last human breath of
the Light of the World?
And did the showbread suddenly go stale
as the true Bread of Life was broken?

I wonder...
what really happened in the temple that day
(the day the veil was torn).

Did the priests realize their work was done
when the perfect High Priest cried,
"It is finished"?

I wonder...
did they run into God's presence
with a shout of thanksgiving?
Or did they scurry about, trying to make
everything function as before,
not comprehending the sacrifice that
brought about God's final satisfaction?

And I wonder...what would I have done?

THE APPLE TREE

"For there is hope of a tree, if it be cut down, that it will sprout again, and that the tender branch thereof will not cease." Job 14:7

They pruned the apple tree today,
the saw wielded,
indiscriminately, it seemed,
tossing to the ground branches
useless, barren, moss-covered.
Now it is only a skeleton,
bare-boned, denuded of leaves and blossoms.
And I feel a little sad.
Necessary, though, was this pruning
and very late in coming.
For years we had said,
"We must prune the apple tree."
But somehow, I still feel a little sad.

And I think as I watch, that right now
I feel like the naked apple tree.
All the beautiful branches I had grown,
the fruit that had been produced and picked,
even what had dropped to the ground, gone.
Gone with the realization
that I have been too busy sprouting
my own blossoms to let God prune me
so I could bear the fruit that would glorify Him.

I feel stripped. Lost, confused.
There are tears in my eyes as I gaze on
the apple tree, and my life.

But I hear His whisper,
His loving whisper,
"Inside the tree is everything needed
to grow more fruit.
Inside you is all I placed there
from the beginning of time."
So I begin to thank Him for the pruning.

The apple tree will bloom again,
and so will I.

TREASURE

"The LORD hath appeared of old unto me, saying, 'Yea, I have loved thee with an everlasting love, therefore with lovingkindness have I drawn thee.'" Jeremiah 31:3

I unwrapped a treasure the other day.
Saved for me by my mother,
wrapped in cotton wool,
reminder of things past,
a memory filled with joy.
Reflecting on my mother
brings my thoughts to You, God,
into Whose hands she placed me
when she went to be with You.
Father, You've said I am your treasure
and so I was thinking of
the protection You provided,
cotton wool placed around me to keep me
from making some horrible mistakes.
Even though I made plenty of them,
left totally on my own I would have
bounced out of the box and broken,
shattering myself into uselessness.
But You covered me with
Your soft cottony love so that one day
You could bring me out
and let me shine for You.

Am I ready yet?

IN HIS KEEPING

"...and I come to thee, Holy Father, keep through thine own name those whom Thou has given me..." John 17:11

"Jude, a bond-servant of Jesus Christ, and brother of James, to those who are the called, beloved in God the Father, and kept for Jesus Christ." Jude 1 (NASB)

I was reading a letter the other day.
Though written two thousand years ago,
it was addressed to me.
Preserved as Holy Scripture,
it speaks volumes to my hungry heart,
letting me know I am beloved, called, kept.
And as I am thinking about
what it means to be kept—
guarded, protected,
held fast in the arms of God—
tears come unbidden as I look back over
my life and know deep in my soul
how steadfastly He has kept me.
I see He is keeping me now and is able
to keep me from stumbling,
from falling into error,
from losing my intimacy with Him;
and all in answer to the prayer
of my Savior when
He asked His Father
to keep me through His name,
because I belong to Him.

Oh, my beloved Lord,
the goal before me is to
keep myself in Your love,
and so my heart cries from
the safety of Your keeping,
To You, and only You,
be all the glory of my life!

HIS HOLY NAME

"Therefore say unto the house of Israel, 'Thus saith the
Lord GOD; I do not this for your sakes, O house of Israel
but mine holy name's sake, which ye have profaned among
the heathen, whither ye went." Ezekiel 36:22

God has restored me,
as long ago He promised
the children of Israel:
not for their sake, nor for mine,
but for the sake of
His holy name.

God has redeemed me,
bought me back with His sacrifice,
set me apart:
not because of my great worth,
but so that I could properly honor
His holy name.

God has renewed me,
placed His Spirit within:
not because of my significance,
but for the purpose
He created me, to bear
His holy name.

God has reclaimed me,
the life that shamed Him,
washed my unclean heart:
just to show to all He is the Lord,
for the sake of
His holy name.

SHADOW AND SUBSTANCE

*"Yea, in the shadow of Your wings will I make my refuge
until these calamities be overpast." Psalm 57:1*

Shadow…
floating, flimsy effigy
of substance.

Yet when calamity
comes against the soul
there is more substance in His shadow
than in any shelter this world can offer.

Oh, God, may I always
face the enemy
from the seclusion
of Your shadow.

VIRTUOSO

"...that the God of our Lord Jesus Christ, the Father of glory, may give unto you the spirit of wisdom and revelation in the knowledge of him; the eyes of your understanding being enlightened; that ye may know what is the hope of his calling, and what the riches of the glory of his inheritance in the saints." Ephesians 1:17, 18

The violinist,
a virtuoso.
Flying fingers expertly
form chords that are
made into music by the
long slow drawing of the bow
across the strings.
Mesmerized,
I watch the fascinating interplay,
my spirit absorbing
the beauty of the sound.

And then, truth sweetly dawns.
This is how God works in me.
Masterful omnipotent fingers
arrange, move, situate,
forming the chords that create music
as He draws His sovereign bow
across the strings of my life.

ON EARTH, IN ME

"And it came to pass, that, as he was praying in a certain place, when he ceased, one of his disciples said unto him. 'Lord, teach us to pray.'" Luke 11:1

Often we murmur the Lord's Prayer,
the words embedded in memory,
spoken in unison with scarcely a thought
of what we are really saying.
It's easy to parrot, "Thy will be done
on earth as it is in heaven."
But what goes on in heaven that
needs to happen on earth?
There, all glory goes to God:
He is the supreme focus, and
everything else pales in the presence
of His majesty.
Is that true in my life?
I wonder how I can pray
"Thy will be done on earth as it is in heaven"
(meaning that all glory is given to You)
if I am not willing to pray
"Thy will be done in *me*, as it is in heaven"?
Am I saying "Work Your will
through everybody else, I will enjoy the benefits?"
Oh, how arrogant!

Father, teach me to pray.

MASTERPIECE

"For I know the plans I have for you," declares the LORD,
"plans to prosper you and not to harm you, plans to give
you hope and a future." Jeremiah 29:11 (NIV)

Sunset wraps the warmth of day
in vibrancy.
Shades of fire explode into
a night
that gives birth
to a silver-frosted dawn.

Masterpieces, originated
by the Creator,
proclaim His glory
in vivid splendor
and icy alabaster.

This Painter of contrasts
is at work in my life too,
desiring that the sunny colors of joy
and the chilly whiteness of pain
together will display His glory.

And though I cannot always
discern the brush strokes,
I know that in both hardship and delight,
He is painting
a masterpiece of love
on the canvas of my heart.

REFLECTION

*"But just as he who called you is holy, so be holy in all you
do; for it is written: 'Be holy, because I am holy.'"*
1 Peter 1:15, 16

Mirrored
in the inlet's glassy sheen,
forested slopes display themselves
in reverse.

As I marvel at the perfection,
an underwater disturbance
creates a ripple,
distorting the image,
and I wonder,
"Jesus, what is it in me that
distorts my reflection
of You?"

I ALWAYS THOUGHT...

"But when he, the Spirit of truth, comes, he will guide you into all truth. He will not speak on his own; he will speak only what he hears, and he will tell you what is yet to come. He will bring glory to me by taking from what is mine and making it known to you." John 16:13, 14 (NIV)

How many times,
when deep in Scripture,
and faced with a new revelation,
do I clutch at my long-held opinions
and, stubbornly resistant, claim
"But, I always thought..."
What an effective set of earplugs
I can wear,
muting the sound of God's voice!
Is it possible that we reject truth
because our minds are plugged
with what is merely an opinion?
My teacher, the Holy Spirit,
must chuckle often when I chime in,
"Is that the truth?
But, I always thought..."

THE SCAFFOLD

*"When you were dead in your sins and in the
uncircumcision of your sinful nature, God made you alive
with Christ. He forgave us all our sins, having canceled
the written code, with its regulations, that was against us
and that stood opposed to us; he took it away, nailing it to
the cross." Colossians 2:13, 14 (NIV)*

Latticework
intricately surrounds
uncompleted buildings.

Scaffolding,
signs of work in progress,
temporary frames to be removed
when labor's done,
purposed to support workmen,
tools, supplies.

High on Calvary's hill
a scaffold stood,
rough timbers supporting
the incarnate tabernacle.
The cross, the ultimate scaffold,
is no longer visible,
yet to eyes of hope,
stands forever as a framework
for the finished task in which
my faith rests.

"And this is love; that we walk in obedience
to his commands."
2 John 6 (NIV)

DO I?

"Sing joyfully to the LORD, you righteous; it is fitting for
the upright to praise him. By the word of the LORD were
the heavens made, their starry host by the breath of his
mouth. He gathers the waters of the sea into jars; he puts
the deep into storehouses. Let all the earth fear the LORD;
let all the people of the world revere him."
Psalm 33:1, 6-8 (NIV)

Tree branches sway to
the music of the wind,
raising in adoration to their Maker.
When I am stirred by His presence,
the Spirit blowing through me
asks me to adore Him.
Do I?

Rain weeps from gray skies,
watering the earth.
Responding growth
gives the Creator glory.
Suffering comes and
tears flood my heart.
When growth responds He only
asks me to give Him glory.
Do I?

Creation praises His majesty.
Heavens blaze, mountains tremble,
birds sing.
And mankind is His
crowning achievement,
I am His creation.

He asks only of me that
I praise Him with my life.
Do I?

He reached down for love of me,
became like me, and gave His life.
Redeemed me, cleansed me, healed me.
I have only to receive.
And all He asks of me is
that I love Him with my heart.
Do I?

AWAKENING

"With my soul have I desired thee in the night; yea, with my spirit within me will I seek thee early; for when thy judgments are in the earth, the inhabitants of the world will learn righteousness." Isaiah 26:9

I overslept this morning.
You awakened me, God,
and I heard You asking me to
spend some time with You.
You, the God of the universe,
desired to talk with me!
But I fluffed my pillow and turned over,
mumbling "Later, God," rebuffing You.
My dreams were twisted, troubling,
and unrested,
I later awakened with no time to pray.

I hurt You this morning, Father.
Even while I accept
the forgiveness You extend as I confess,
I mourn the loss that is mine
in granting my selfish desire.
The truth is,
strength and energy, joy and purpose
come from You,
not from another hour of sleep.

What treasure might I have discovered
if I had only answered the soft ringing
of Your alarm clock?

FALLOW GROUND

"Sow to yourselves in righteousness, reap in mercy; break up your fallow ground; for it is time to seek the LORD, until he come and rain righteousness upon you."
Hosea 10:12

For a while my field's been empty.
Fallow ground,
unplowed, unplanted.
Dormant,
though becoming fertile.
Lord, plow my heart
and plant your seed.
Let the crop be rich, abundant,
with a harvest produced
with patience,
cultivated, reaped to show
that seeds of faith and love
can grow from earth
that has lain fallow.

EXPECTANCY

"My soul, wait thou only upon God; for my expectation is from him." Psalm 62:5

It is spring.
Each glance out of the window is delight.
I watch the robins that flock together
on my lawn,
eagerly seeking sustenance,
fully expecting results.

Fascinating how they hop determinedly
to a spot where perhaps they detect the
slight tremor of earth that indicates
the slithering passage of a worm.
Alert, heads cocked, listening,
they sense an end to their quest
and are filled with hope.
Robins have much to teach me
if I would stop and learn.
Am I living in eager expectation?
Do I stop, listen, and seek out the food
God has for me?
Do I approach Him with confidence;
a hope that has certainty of fulfillment?
How about anticipation?
Is there a longing for
the pleasure of His company?

Little robin, you are doing exactly
what you were created to do.
Am I?

THE VOICE

"...and behold the LORD passed by, and a great and strong wind rent the mountains, and brake in pieces the rocks before the LORD; but the LORD was not in the wind; and after the wind an earthquake, but the LORD was not in the earthquake; and after the earthquake a fire; but the LORD was not in the fire; and after the fire a still small voice."
1 Kings 19:11-12

Feeling bereft sometimes
when I have done all the things
I supposed I must do to please God,
and He seems so far away,
I stand complaining,
"Where are You, God?

Your still, small voice,
a gentle whisper...
do I seek it in a whirlwind,
a flurry of activity?

Your still, small voice,
a gentle whisper...
is it audible in the earth-quaking changes
I try to make in my world?

Your still, small voice,
a gentle whisper...
can I hear it in the fire
of my zeal to do His work?

Your still, small voice,
a gentle whisper...
is it drowned out by
the clamor of flapping wings
as I try to fly alone?

Do I need a hearing aid?

BABY STEPS

"The LORD preserveth the simple; I was brought low, and he helped me. Return unto thy rest, O my soul; for the LORD hath dealt bountifully with thee. For thou hast delivered my soul from death, mine eyes from tears and my feet from falling. I will walk before the LORD in the land of the living." Psalm 116:6-9

Our granddaughter is walking!
So small,
it seems she has deserted our laps too early.
So determined,
for weeks she has pulled herself up
on every available piece of furniture,
testing her leg strength,
taking a tentative step, then two.
So focused,
her attention unwavering on her destination,
she fearlessly toddles forth.
What joy I feel when she launches herself
into my arms after a wobbly run
across the space between us!

So I've been thinking, as I watch her,
of God drawing us to Himself.
We wobble and hesitate,
needing to be held, carried,
picked up when we fall.
Experiencing Him infuses divine strength
into our baby steps,
our legs of faith empowered.

God has carried me for so long.
Still testing my legs, I often fall.
He wants my focus on Him,
my limbs to strengthen.
Not, though, so I can stand alone,
but run straight into His arms.

PILLARS

*"By day the LORD went ahead of them in a pillar of cloud
to guide them on their way and by night in a pillar of fire to
give them light, so that they could travel by day or night."
Exodus 13:21 (NIV)*

I was reading today
about the children of Israel
and their wilderness wandering.
Nomads, homeless, they were set apart
from the surrounding peoples
by God's visible presence:
a pillar of fire by night,
a pillar of cloud by day.
What a wonder it must have been!
Did the sight strike awe
into hearts of the watchers,
unaware of who really
inhabited those pillars?
There was never any doubt that
something was different
about the Israelites.

I was wondering about my own life.
Are the pillars of God's presence
visible to people who observe me?
Do I shine in the darkness around me?
Am I surrounded by a cloud of His fragrance?

Oh, God, please inhabit me in such a way
that no one will doubt
that something is different about me.

CANAAN

*"...the Israelites groaned in their slavery and cried out,
and their cry for help because of their slavery went up to
God. God heard their groaning and He remembered His
covenant with Abraham, Isaac and Jacob. So God looked
on the Israelites and was concerned about them."
Exodus 2:23-25 (NIV)*

In my bondage, do I crave deliverance,
or simply relief from burdens?
Do I yearn for the Promised Land or,
mired in captivity's comfort,
tamp down the desire,
the vague stirrings of hunger
for something once known?

For buried deep within is a memory
of the perfection of Eden
planted in my soul at conception,
so far below my conscious thought
it merely registers a soul-deep longing.
I have spent so many years of my life
in stunted expectation.

God, as You did so long ago
for Your children,
call my heart to liberation.
Please give again the promise of Eden.
Re-awaken the desire for Canaan
that I may follow my Deliverer
in trembling awe
through the wilderness
to my true home.

DELIVERANCE

"...and there you will serve gods, the work of men's hands,
wood and stone, which neither see nor hear nor eat nor
smell. But from there you will seek the LORD your God,
and you will find Him if you search for Him with all your
heart and all your soul." Deuteronomy 4:28-29 (NASB)

Scattered among ruins,
my hardened heart expels me
from the side of God,
thrusting into sin,
stubbornly refusing to capitulate
to the Voice that rules the universe
and the whisper brushing His plea
across my soul,
"Seek Me."

He does not give up, does not retreat,
as I worship at the shrine of self,
the work of my hands.
He simply calls, and I begin to hear His promise
"But from there, out there where
you are struggling, you will look for me
and I will be found.
Bring your heart, your seeking soul, to Me
and I will carry you back to Canaan,
the place of intimacy and rest."

The longing, the desire, build and swell
until my stubborn heart is broken and I cry,
"My compassionate Lord,
my covenant God,
receive, revive me, restore me.

And You will.
Because You are Jehovah
and You do not forget."

NOW THEREFORE ARISE

"Moses My servant is dead; now therefore arise, cross this Jordan, you and all this people, to the land which I am giving to them, to the sons of Israel." Joshua 1:2 (NASB)

God's children stood poised
at the entrance to the Promised Land.
Moses, their leader, was gone.
Mourning, they hesitated, accustomed
to the wandering,
living with the "someday" hope.
But someday is here
and Joshua hears the voice,
"now therefore arise, and enter."
God didn't, however, push His children:
He walked with them,
promising never
to leave them,
nor fail them.

I am wondering if I am mired
in accustomed sameness,
nursing my past, mourning my losses,
stuck in the desert of comfort.
Is God saying "Now therefore arise" to me?
Whether it is a physical, emotional or
spiritual transition I am to make
(or all three),
I do not enter it alone.

He impels me with His command,
strengthens my courage
with His presence,
and nourishes my soul
with His word.

I think it's time to move.

FAR-AWAY HEARTS

"The LORD says 'These people come near to me with their mouth and honor me with their lips, but their hearts are far from me. Their worship of me is made up only of rules taught by men.'" Isaiah 29:13 (NIV)

When God says,
"Draw near to Me",
we approach,
our gifts of service held out in eager hands.
Singing hymns, speaking prayers
with saintly lips we say,
"Look what I've done for You."
Others look and see.
We preen,
so pleased our sacrifice is noted.

Then God says again,
"Draw near to Me.
Your lips honor me,
but your hearts are far away,
encased in bonds of self-serving pride."

When next we hear God say,
"Draw near to Me",
may we take our broken hearts
and lay them at His feet.
Pleased, He'll bind them up and heal them,
a sacrifice received.

FIRST PLACE

"Speak unto the children of Israel, and bid them that they
make them fringes in the borders of their garments
throughout their generations, and that they put upon the
fringe of the borders a ribband of blue." Numbers 15:38

A ribbon of blue, worn to remind
God's people to live in holy obedience.
I guess it's no surprise, then,
that we reward excellence with the same symbol.

One day I received a blue ribbon.
My hard work had produced
an item worthy of a prize,
judged to be the best.
My pride knew no bounds,
and for years the ribbon
graced my memory's wall.
Now it lies dusty and faded
among the relics of the past.

So I am thinking today, am I living holy,
giving Jesus first place?
Do I put the time and energy
into our relationship
as I did my blue-ribbon project?
I want Him to be as thrilled with me
as I was when the judge
gave me a blue ribbon,
so maybe I should pull out
that frayed prize
and hang it up again as a reminder

of all the work He did for me;
and obediently name Him
as the One in my life
who has first place.

EXTRAVAGANCE

"Charge them that are rich in this world, that they be not high-minded, nor trust in riches, but in the living God, who giveth us richly all things to enjoy." 1 Timothy 6:17

"And I will very gladly spend and be spent for you..."
2 Corinthians 12:15

My wallet is empty.
Just this morning it was filled
with crisp bills and jingling coins.
Now there is nothing,
and not much to show in exchange
for my spending,
just a few odds and ends
that attracted my desires.
I spent it all on myself.

As with my wallet, I think,
so it goes with my life.
God spent lavishly on me
but I don't seem to share His essence
with others.
How can I, with the knowledge
of His love for me,
be unwilling to be spent, to be poured out?
I clutch the blessing tightly,
spending it all on myself.

Please, Lord,
remake me into one
who spends your love,
extravagantly,
on others.

WITHHOLDING TAX

"Withhold not thou thy tender mercies from me, O LORD:
let thy truth continually preserve me." Psalm 40:11

I feel my face tighten in anger and hurt.
Someone has damaged my feelings
and I retreat in withdrawal.
Holding back my affection and,
curling into a familiar defensive position,
my joy suppressed,
I have an unholy practice of
selfishly withholding my self from others.

But I was just thinking,
what if Jesus withheld Himself
whenever I hurt or disappointed Him?
What if He pulled back His love, His mercy,
His offer of forgiveness?

It would be a withholding tax
that would rob me of everything
to pay.

UNVEILING

*"But when He who had set me apart, even from my
mother's womb, and called me through His grace, was
pleased to reveal His Son in me..." Galatians 1:15, 16*

Is Jesus revealed in me?
Or am I so covered up
with self-promoting achievement
that the clarity of His presence is
hidden by smoked glass?
Perhaps there is an outline of His shape,
a glimmer of His light,
but do I reveal Him?

He called me, saved me,
not only because of His great love,
but so He could be seen through me,
so I would shine for Him.
I wonder, though,
if I have not drawn the filmy curtains
of self-gratification across the windows of my life,
reveling in my deeds,
rather than revealing His loveliness.

Please,
unveil Your glory in me, Lord:
Be revealed.

PUNCTUATION

"...and though you have not seen Him, you love Him, and though you do not see Him now, but believe in Him, you greatly rejoice with joy inexpressible and full of glory."
1 Peter 1:8

True joy
is the exclamation point
that ends the sentence
"I will!"
It is
complete surrender
to
Jesus Christ.

COMPARISON

"And we, who with unveiled faces all reflect the Lord's glory, are being transformed into his likeness with ever-increasing glory, which comes from the Lord, who is the Spirit." 2 Corinthians 3:18 (NIV)

Seated on a fallen log,
the beauty of nature surrounding me,
I happened to glance up to see
an eagle perched high in a tree.
He was peering at me intently,
at least so it seemed.
While I marveled at the power
and majesty of its existence,
somehow I felt uncomfortable
as the object of its scrutiny.

Then one day I caught myself
perched high in the tree
of spiritual superiority,
gazing disparagingly upon another,
and I remembered the eagle.
Stunned, I realized that
looking down upon others
is an uncomfortable perch
when I look up into the face of
the One to Whom
I should be conforming.

I have no doubt
that He sees the comparison.

IN THE STRUGGLE

"But he giveth more grace. Wherefore he saith, God resisteth the proud, but giveth grace unto the humble. Submit yourselves therefore to God." James 4:6-7

Father, I want You to be pre-eminent in my life.
So why do I fight so hard to bring about *my* goals?
It's rather like the condition of my bed
after a sleepless night;
sheets and blankets crumpled, twisted,
evidence of struggle against the letting-go of sleep.
Or like my knitting after a series of mistakes;
knotted and messy.

God, that's what I do to my life.
You long for me to rest in you.
You'll keep the sheets smooth when I lie still.
And if I would knit more slowly,
paying attention to the instructions,
there wouldn't be tight knots,
or ruined yarn from frustrated pulling.

Yet, even as I learn Your lessons, I realize,
there is growth in the struggle,
that to survive I need
the strength You provide
as a by-product of our tussle;
and I understand
that inertia brings defeat
but surrender brings victory.

INK

"And to know the love of Christ, which passeth knowledge,
that ye might be filled with all the fullness of God."
Ephesians 3:19

I love to write with a fountain pen.
Sliding smoothly over the paper,
all is well until the pen begins to run dry.
Frustrated, I press harder, shaking it,
trying to eke one more sentence
from a pen with nothing left.
Unwilling to get up and fill the pen,
I often lay it down,
my writing abandoned.

I wonder if my life
isn't sometimes like the pen,
running dry because
I haven't replenished
the ink cartridge
from my prayer closet.
Is God shaking me,
pressing me harder
to let me know He can't use me
when I am drained?

How can God write His message of love
through me if I only offer Him a pen
empty of ink?

SOFTENING

*"Let my teaching fall like rain and my words descend like
dew, like showers on new grass, like abundant rain on
tender plants." Deuteronomy 32:2 (NIV)*

Sometimes, Lord,
I'm like a dry sponge—
hard, useless.
Drop by drop, please
pour Your word into me,
'til the living water is absorbed
and I become soft, usable
for my created purpose,
and every pore is seeping;
so when I am squeezed,
from the sponge will flow
the abundance of a life
filled with You.

CLEANSING

"Have mercy on me, O God, according to Your unfailing love; according to Your great compassion blot out my transgressions. Wash away all my iniquity and cleanse me from my sin. Create in me a new heart, O God, and renew a steadfast spirit within me." Psalm 51:1, 2, 10 (NIV)

Newly washed by gentle rain,
creation sparkles.
Unmatched colors, intensely vivid,
glow in the crystal air.
Each leaf, each bough, each blossom
and distant mountain peak,
distinct.

Was it so long ago my heart,
newly washed by the outpouring
of living water, saw with vivid clarity
colors of the future gleaming with promise?
A dusty cloud, complacency,
obscures my vision now and dims
the brightness in my soul.
I long to gaze on You with wonder.

Lord, wash me again.

LEANING

"The eternal God is thy refuge, and underneath are the everlasting arms." Deuteronomy 33:27

One never leans
with expectation of falling;
the very act of leaning
is one of faith and trust.

I want to lean on God.
My head tells me He will not fail
but I don't seem to let go and lean.
From where comes my fear of falling?
From where comes the tightness of the grip
that says holding on to this world
supports me more completely than God?

I think there is no way to learn to lean
than simply to lean.

THE OFFERING

"As he looked up, Jesus saw the rich putting their gifts into the temple treasury. He also saw a poor widow put in two very small copper coins. 'I tell you the truth', he said, 'this poor widow has put in more than all the others.'"
Luke 21:1-4 (NIV)

Standing at the altar, a token in my hand,
I wait for the smile of approval
I feel is sure to come.
It is much more than I usually bring.
I know God must be pleased
with my offering.

Another approaches the altar
whose offering seems
not nearly as big as mine,
and I scoff, my pride eclipsing the
truth of sacrifice until, hearing the words
"It's all I have, but it's Yours",
I am undone.

I have brought an offering,
she has offered everything.
And I think how I have tried to appease
my Savior with a drop
of what He has given me when
He poured out every drop
of His blood for me.

Appease Him?
Or abandon all to Him?
That is His charge to me...
my challenge,
and my choice.

INTO CAPTIVITY

*"For the weapons of our warfare are not carnal, but mighty
through God to the pulling down of strong holds; casting
down imaginations, and every high thing that exalteth itself
against the knowledge of God, and bringing into captivity
every thought to the obedience of Christ."*
2 Corinthians 10:4-5

My sinful thoughts,
so much a part of me;
familiar, those reactions,
thrusting sharp sword points into
the tender armor of
my new intimacy with God.

An altercation begins,
my thoughts against His,
the old against the new
on the battlefield of my mind.
Coexistence is impossible,
defeat of one or the other inevitable.

I choose the weapons,
the fiery darts of the evil one
bringing envy and bitterness
to the front lines,
or the spiritual Sword,
mighty through God,
able to pierce my darkness.
Here on my knees the battle rages.
I have heard of, read of,
and even known in the past,
the victory available
over the foe that is me,

but obedience is hard.
God, please soften my heart
with willingness to break the bondage
and bring every thought
into captivity.

CONSTANT SURRENDER

*"I am crucified with Christ; nevertheless I live; yet not I
but Christ liveth in me; and the life which I now live in the
flesh I live by the faith of the Son of God, who loved me and
gave himself for me," Galatians 2:20*

I asked you, Jesus, into my heart,
then dragged You with me where I wanted to go,
resisting the gentle tugging
suggesting a better way.
Wasn't it enough that you dwelt there?

You provided me a way to heaven.
I thought that's why I needed You.
Though unwilling to turn over control,
I climbed aboard salvation's ship and
blithely sailed off to live the Christian life.

But You want more.
You want the helm,
willingly surrendered.
How many times I've sung
"I Surrender All"
without knowing its meaning
in the depths of my soul.

All that is me;
my hopes and dreams, plans and schemes,
must come under Your guiding hand
in constant surrender.

BACKWASH

"Finally, all of you, live in harmony with one another; be sympathetic, love as brothers, be compassionate and humble. Do not repay evil with evil or insult with insult, but with blessing, because to this you were called so that you may inherit a blessing." 1 Peter 3:8, 9 (NIV)

The ship pushes forward through the waves,
determined, its destination firmly fixed.
Fueled to perform its appointed task,
piloted with ambition, it is programmed
to complete the mission.
I stand at the stern, staring at the frothy wake
churned by massive propellers,
musing on the power
that creates such agitation.
Suddenly a small boat crosses the wake,
bouncing nearly out of control
in the backwash of the ship.

My thoughts turn inward and
I ponder my own wake.
Pressing unheeding toward my goals,
do I churn up froth, making waves
that embroil those about me in distress; and I,
programmed to complete my mission, sail on?

Oh, God, may I look around
for the smaller boats,
and slow down in my passing
so that crossing my wake will not cause them
to be tossed about,
or frightened,
or lost.

BROOMS

*"If we confess our sins, He is faithful and just to forgive us
our sin and cleanse us from all unrighteousness."*
1 John 1:9

I swept the floor clean of debris this morning.
I did it yesterday morning,
and I will do it again tomorrow.
It is autumn, wet outdoors,
and somehow a constant stream of dirt
tracks itself across my floor.
And I wonder, why am I sweeping so vigorously
when I know it will be clean for such a short time?
Why do I do it over and over and over?

Somehow I can hear God's voice
nudging me and I remember how many times
He has swept me clean,
knowing that before much time has elapsed
there will be dirt tracks across my heart
and I will have to come running to Him
and ask to be cleaned up again.
How can He do it over and over and over?

Because He promised.
And perhaps the joy of a restored relationship
sparkling like new
brings satisfaction to Him,
something like my momentarily clean floor
brings me. So I sweep, and praise Him…
and sweep, and thank Him
for His broom of love that never rests,
but ever waits to whisk the mud
from the floor of my heart.

MEMORY

"Remember, O LORD, thy tender mercies and thy
lovingkindnesses; for they have been ever of old.
Remember not the sins of my youth, nor my transgression;
according to thy mercy remember thou me for thy
goodness' sake, O LORD." Psalm 25:6, 7

Memory weaves a fabric,
a tapestry telling a story.
My God and I together examine
the design and I am enthralled
with the threads that show
His faithfulness to
remember His covenant.
The God of the universe,
Who created me,
Who formed me,
says He will forever remember me.

I ponder His benefits,
our relationship deepens.
I say, "Father, remember when?"
He responds, "Ah, yes and do you remember…?"

So I consider the texture He weaves
into my memory and my heart lifts in praise,
for I remember something else He said,
under the new covenant in Christ's blood,
He will remember my sins
no more forever!

GOODBYE

"But now you must rid yourselves of all such things as these: anger, rage, malice, slander, and filthy language from your lips. Do not lie to each other, seeing you have taken off your old self with its practices; and have put on the new self, which is being renewed in knowledge in the image of its Creator." Colossians 3:8-10 (NIV)

She wouldn't wave goodbye, no hug or kiss.
Instead she buried her head
in her daddy's shoulder
and only peeked as we drove away.
I longed for one more "I love you, Grandma.
I will miss you."
No coaxing, no pleading, deterred her.
So we drove away.
Disappointed a bit, rather than hurt,
and puzzled, because it had been such a good visit,
I began thinking that in her child's heart
the acts of hugging, kissing and waving
bring to reality the leaving,
the parting and goodbye.
And I hoped it was so.

Then I wondered about some things in my life
that need to be gone.
Do I hold on to them sometimes
by my refusal to kiss them goodbye?
Hoping, somehow, that I won't have to let go.
I just hide my eyes,
knowing the necessity of repentance,
yet standing stubbornly in my own way.

Oh, God, forgive me.
Renew me.
Remake me.

A THANKFUL HEART

*"In everything give thanks, for this is the will of God in
Christ Jesus concerning you" 1 Thessalonians 5:18*

Help me to remember sunshine's blaze
when rain drops endless fall.
Help me remember the joyful days
when sorrow comes to call.
And that often there awaits a rosy dawn
when a night has been especially long.

Lord, please help me understand
Your plans seldom mesh with mine.
Teach me to trust and clasp Your hand
in joy or sorrow, and let me find
the Power that shapes and molds
my days is the Power that upholds.

Lord, help me see that You are near,
and all comes from your hand.
In trial and triumph, faith and fear
let me be thankful, for Your demand,
when through grace my life is viewed,
is only a heart of gratitude.

HOME

*"He longed to fill his stomach with the pods that the pigs
were eating...when he came to his senses, he said, 'I will
set out and go back to my father'. So he got up and went to
his father. But while he was still a long way off, his father
saw him and was filled with compassion for him; he ran to
his son, threw his arms around him and kissed him."
Luke 15:16a, 17a, 18-20 (NIV)*

Hunger, a driving force,
sends me foraging to fill the empty depths,
strangling on cornhusks, parched and dry,
gleanings of my rebellious harvest.
Still the hunger gnaws,
and I can find nothing more
where I am wandering so far from home.

Do I hear the splashing of clear water,
detect the scent of verdant pasture,
sense the peace of a heart restored?
Home awaits.

Where do you forage to feed
the cravings of your soul?
Rooting through earth's refuse
seeking morsels to keep hunger at bay?
This world has no nourishment
for the child of God.
Come home.
Your Father awaits.

THE PARTY

"One of them, when he saw he was healed, came back
praising God in a loud voice. He threw himself at Jesus'
feet and thanked him..." Luke 17:15, 16 (NIV)

I went to a party yesterday.
Surprise! It was for me!
There were no bounds to my gratitude
and my heart ached with the inability
to express the joy.
I wanted to sing and dance and shout
that someone cared,
cared enough to prepare this gift,
just for me.

Then this morning I was chastened
by the realization that
I'm invited to another party—
it's called eternity, and it, too, is for me!
I *am* grateful, but why am I not singing,
dancing and shouting that
Someone cared enough to prepare
the gift of life for me?

I want my heart to ache with the desire
to express my joy,
and let everyone know they, too,
are invited to the party.

HEAVEN

*"For the grace of God that brings salvation has appeared
to all men. It teaches us to say 'No' to ungodliness and
worldly passions, and to live self-controlled, upright and
godly lives in this present age, while we wait for the blessed
hope—the glorious appearing of our great God and Savior
Jesus Christ." Titus 2:11-13 (NIV)*

My lawn,
a frustrating series of dirt mounds
produced by burrowing creatures who dwell
in the darkness below;
the piles the only evidence of
infrequent surfacing for air.
I am irritated by their ugly presence,
but God speaks a lesson to my heart,
as another picture fills my mind
and I am once again a little girl
happily playing outside,
the grass cool between my bare toes.
As the shining sun begins
to dip over the hill,
I hear the call from Daddy
to come home for dinner,
and I run and leap into his arms
to be carried to the table.

I don't want to tunnel through this life,
seeing only the darkness surrounding me.
I want my days to be filled
with childlike expectancy,
my ears alert for God's voice.

And though my feet still touch the grass of earth,
may my hands be raised toward heaven,
ready to be lifted in my Father's arms
and be carried home to dinner.

VISTA

"For here have we no continuing city, but we seek one to come." Hebrews 13:14

Thirty floors up, I have a vantage point
from which to peer at the city.
Surrounded by concrete, glass and steel,
people and things,
I am embraced by its reality,
yet I am only visiting.
Situated here, I can also see
between the buildings
across the water the mountains
where I live.
It is a lovely vista, and my eyes
are drawn away from the city
to its pristine panorama.

I was thinking, Father,
that's how it is with us,
pilgrims on earth,
caught in the web of this world.
Distracted by its pleasures,
we huddle beneath its skyscrapers,
scurry along its sidewalks,
intent upon survival within its boundaries,
when You want to lift us up to look
between the buildings at heaven's vista
which beckons and
calls us home.

THE ENGAGEMENT

"Love the Lord your God with all your heart and with all your soul and with all your mind and with all your strength." Mark 12:30 (NIV)

All my strength, my passion.
Passion infuses strength,
passivity enables weakness.
God desires my passion because
He is passionate about me.
I remember my engagement ring
and how I would wave my hand dramatically
at every opportunity so that people would
see it and ask about my fiancé.
Eloquently, passionately,
describing the wonder of my love,
I was unable to be passive.

So I am thinking that I am
part of the bride of Christ,
falling in love with Him.
Am I passionate about Him?
Living in such expectancy that I want
to tell everyone about the wonder
of His love for me?

May His engagement diamond
sparkle from my eyes,
shine through my life,
so that people will ask about Him,
Jesus, my Savior,
and I will proclaim Him,
passionately,
with all my strength.

BRIDAL GOWN

"Let us be glad and rejoice, and give honor to Him; for the
marriage of the Lamb is come, and his bride has made
herself ready. And to her was granted that she should be
arrayed in fine linen, clean and white; for the fine linen is
the righteousness of saints." Revelation 19:8

I've been working on my wedding dress
with great excitement.
I know the day is nearing
and my gown must be ready.

My pattern (the radiant Christ) is beautiful,
and I'm endeavoring to cut the
fabric of clean white linen to His design.

The walk down the aisle, I know,
is only a twinkling of an eye,
so I'm not sewing this gown
for the admiration of the guests,
I will be wearing it only
for my Bridegroom.

And as I stitch, my entire being throbs
in anticipation for the moment
when He lifts the veil
and I will see His face.

"But I will hope continually, and will yet praise
thee more and more."
Psalm 71:14

REAL WORDS

"O Lord, open thou my lips; and my mouth shall show forth thy praise" Psalm 51:15

Quiet, for just a moment, she nestles in my lap,
the picture book open;
I am trying to teach her words.
It isn't often that she is still enough,
and I long for her to begin to exchange baby talk
for real communication.
She smiles and points to the page,
"Kitty," she says plainly.
I am beside myself! She is saying words!

Thinking of how I had been asking God
to reveal His desire for me
to commune with Him,
I am amazed at the beauty and clarity
of His answer.

Can't I picture myself
nestled on His lap,
His book opened before us?
He points to His words
and asks me to speak to Him.
Cannot I then understand His joy
when I grasp truth and
respond with my own words,
fresh from new comprehension?

Communication has begun,
and somehow I hear Him
laughing with delight,
"She is finally saying real words!"

FIRST LOVE

"Nevertheless I have somewhat against thee, because thou hast left thy first love." Revelation 2:4

First love, thrilling in its newness,
filling all spaces in the heart,
flowing out in word and deed all around.
Not to be contained, it is expressed in total joy.

The church at Ephesus, according to Jesus,
left its first love, dismissed its importance,
moving ahead with rigid deeds,
joy extinguished by rules.

I know what that is like.
I left my first love,
wandered for years in the graveyard
of legal standards, wearing a mask of piety,
dead to joy.
Each time I would read of Ephesus
my shame would stab me and
grief would surface, for a moment.

But God, in infinite patience
and compassion,
walked among the rules
with which I'd replaced Him,
drawing me, holding me, wanting only
my unreserved love.
Slowly I watched the veil
pulled away to reveal His face,
heard His poignant plea just for me.
I never knew the depths of joy
my soul could hold

until I unburdened my broken heart
and confessed I had left my first love,
but now,
I have returned!

WORSHIP

"O come, let us worship and bow down; let us kneel before the LORD our maker. For he is our God." Psalm 95:5-6

All that I think of myself is presented
in the appearance of my face, my deeds.
How do I look to God?
But all that He wants of me
must be presented in the nape of my neck,
bowing, surrendered,
vulnerable, trusting, defenseless.

Faith is what it takes for the courage
to bow completely,
abandoned to obedience.

Many are the forms of outward worship.
My hands may be clapping, raised,
or clasped in prayer.
Standing or kneeling,
it is not the position of my body
but the position of my heart
that matters to God;
standing upright in pride
or bowed, face to the ground,
humbled by Holiness.

CLOAKED IN PRAISE

"To appoint unto them that mourn in Zion, to give unto them beauty for ashes, the oil of joy for mourning, the garment of praise for the spirit of heaviness; that they might be called trees of righteousness, the planting of the LORD, that he might be glorified." Isaiah 61:3

So many times when my spirit
is cast down, praise is far
from my stubborn lips.
I'm prostrate with misery,
silence surrounding me like a tomb.

A cloak of praise for my heavy heart,
woven at heaven's loom, awaits,
but I don't move.
Amid the ashes of my despair
I have some comfort in this womb.

Lord, may I fix my eyes upon the robe,
and long to claim it for my own.
Then, please wrap it around me
with your love;
it must be more than mere costume.

Thus clad by your strength
I'll begin once again
my offering of praise,
and trust it will rise
to your throne, a sweet perfume.

RUSH TO PETITION

*"Sing joyfully to the LORD, you righteous; it is fitting for
the upright to praise him." Psalm 33:1 (NIV)*

*"If we confess our sins, he is faithful and just to forgive us
our sins and cleanse us from all unrighteousness."
1 John 1:9*

*"Be careful for nothing, but in everything by prayer and
supplication, with thanksgiving, let our requests be known
unto God." Philippians 4:6*

Bypassing praise,
I dash headlong into God's presence.
Where is the reverent awe?
I wonder if I truly sense His power and greatness.

A placating confession
because I know I must,
but would a mumbled "forgive me" be enough
if I were to look deeply into His face
and really see my sin?

Omitting thanksgiving,
because my tendency is to overlook
His wonders as though the blessings
of my life were my due,

I rush to petition,
finding my voice full and strong.
Needs of others, the lost and hurting,
receive a cursory plea; importance dimmed
in my strident demands.

I know I have the freedom, and confidence
to approach my God, but maybe heeding
His instructions on prayer more seriously
would make my petitions not quite so urgent
in the midst of sweet fellowship.

And then, I think I wouldn't want to rush.

EYES ONLY

"Unto thee, O Lord, do I lift up my soul." Psalm 25:1

Only your eyes, Father,
can see my depths:
only eyes of faith can begin
to penetrate Yours.

But when I pray,
I know my eyes are darting
here, there and everywhere,
lighting for a moment on a need,
a concern, a desire.
Have I lost the secret of delight
in Your presence?
Please help me narrow my focus
and widen my vision
to receive the
revelation of You, Yourself,
personal and confidential.

PRAYER

*"We having the same spirit of faith, according as it is
written, I believed, and therefore have I spoken; we also
believe, and therefore speak." 2 Corinthians 4:13*

Prayer is more about what we are
than all the words we say.
Words are barren, useless things
when our lives are an empty display
of unbelief and selfish hearts;
God's laws ignored day after day.

Prayer begins when a willing heart
confesses sin, heeding the way
He commands. To have faith is to hear,
to hear is to believe, to believe is then to obey.
To obey is to know, to know is to love,
to breathe that love is to pray.

RICHES

*"O LORD, how manifold are thy works! In wisdom hast
thou made them all; the earth is full of thy riches.
Psalm 104:24*

Pine branches sweep green brush strokes
across a silver sky.
"How Great Thou Art", my soul sings with joy.
Heart leaping, beating fast, I think it's excitement.
Could real praise actually feel this way?
Towering spires of tree trunks point to heaven,
carrying my attention to God,
my Creator, my Sustainer,
Who holds it all together,
Who holds *me* together,
and my entire being fills and swells
with awareness of
uncountable blessings,
immeasurable care,
unsearchable greatness!
I bow beneath such riches.

MAJESTY

"Give unto the LORD the glory due unto His name;
worship the Lord in the beauty of holiness." Psalm 29:2

The sky reaches far overhead,
a dazzling azure bowl.
It is all I can see.

The waters of the lake are buoyant,
holding me, and I am astounded anew
with the majesty of God
Who stretched out the sky,
Who rules over the universe.
I am humbled at His immensity,
my puniness.

Then a sound intrudes on the silence.
It is the beat of my heart in my ears.
It is all I can hear,
and I am suddenly significant,
a part of His creation,
the throbbing pulse of my body
proof of His care for me,
my worth to Him as His child.

It is a holy moment.
I worship Him.
It is all I can do.

EPIPHANY

"And he said, 'I beseech thee, show me thy glory.'"
Exodus 33:18

I asked God
to show Himself to me.

He did.

And,
wrapped in wonder,
my heart
saw His face.

BAREFOOT

"And the captain of the Lord's host said unto Joshua,
'Loose thy shoe from off thy foot; for the place whereon
thou standest is holy." Joshua 5:15

I hear You, God,
in the whispering wind,
feel you as the sun kisses my cheek,
see you in the rushing river.

I hear you, God,
in the voice of my husband,
feel You in the embrace of my children,
see You in the growth of my family.

I hear You, God,
in soaring anthems,
feel You in the sanctuary,
see You in the acts of love of Your people.

I hear You, God,
in the cries of the lost and broken,
feel You in the wrenching reality of pain,
see You in the eyes of a hungry child.

Oh, let me fully sense Your nearness,
know that all around is holy ground,
and I will stand before You,
barefoot.

FULLNESS

"Bless the LORD, O my soul, and all that is within me,
bless His holy name. Bless the LORD, O my soul and forget
not all His benefits: who forgives all your iniquities; who
heals all your diseases; who redeems your life from
destruction; who crowns you with lovingkindness and
tender mercies." Psalm 103:1-4

I saw You afresh this morning, Father,
tender with me.
I felt You afresh this morning,
surrounding me in love.
I never realized how hard I was
struggling to please You,
so You wouldn't reject me,
accepting Your judgment,
refusing your tenderness.

My head knowledge of You refuted this,
but tears erupted from my depths today
when the Scripture spoke
of Your loving mercies,
and I was suddenly
aware of my wounded heart,
touched at a primal point of need...
opening, receiving, rejoicing!
I think I have begun to let You love me.

Letting go of the terror
that has gripped my life,
I'm learning to live in
fearless fullness.

STRANGE FIRE

"And Nadab and Abihu, the sons of Aaron, took either of them his censer, and put fire therein, and put incense thereon, and offered strange fire before the LORD, which he commanded them not. And there went out fire from the LORD, and devoured them, and they died before the LORD." Leviticus 10:1, 2

Wounded, proud, considering himself wise,
man stands in bold defiance against his Maker.
He offers strange fire, burning incense
to the idol he's created, forbidden incense,
mixed of high sounding phrases
of praise to himself.
Misplaced worship, pagan in desire,
unholy in practice.
God is not pleased with strange fire.

Oh, Lord God, my heart is fixed on You,
my Creator Sustainer.
May my sacrifice of praise
be burned in your purifying fire,
the sweet savor of a surrendered life
my acceptable worship.
Purge me of anger, of centeredness in self.

Take my pain, I'm wounded, too.
Sprinkle my tears as blood on Your altar.
And as I rest there in Christ's sacrifice,
kindle a flame that will never turn to
strange fire.

FLESH, BONE, SINEW, BREATH

"Thus says the Lord GOD to these bones, 'Behold, I will
cause breath to enter you that you may come to life. And I
will put sinews on you, make flesh grow back on you, cover
you with skin, and put breath in you that you may come
alive and you will know that I am the LORD."
Ezekiel 37:5, 6 (NASB)

By the word of the Lord, by His spirit,
dry bones will live again.
The prophet speaks to me,
as well as to his people Israel,
my life a rattle of dry bones,
undone, piled in a useless heap.

God's message is new life.
Bones to be re-fleshed,
tattered sinews with strength renewed,
skin re-stretched to bind it all together,
and breath, eternal holy breath
brought from the four winds by
the Sovereign Lord, restores my life,
draws me from my self-dug grave,
and now I know, my Father,
You are the LORD!

PSALM

"And when He has thus spoken, He cried with a loud voice, 'Lazarus, come forth.' And he that was dead came forth, bound hand and foot with graveclothes, and his face was bound about with a napkin. Jesus saith unto them, 'Loose him, and let him go.'" John 11:43, 44

I love You, Lord, because
You first loved me.
I will praise You forever because
You cared for me, wept for me,
called me up from the tomb
made of my fears and pain,
and have turned me loose
to fly and be free, to be me.

You have unwrapped the strips
of burial cloth, removed the veil
so I can see Your face.
Let me never turn again
from the certainty of Your love
for me as I am;
because You formed me, shaped me,
breathed my life into me.

Let my outward breath ever be
praise to You,
God of my salvation,
Lord of my life,
Father of my heart.

I AM

*"These are the words of him who is the First and the Last,
who died and came to life again, 'I know your afflictions
and your poverty ... do not be afraid of what you are about
to suffer ... Be faithful, even to the point of death, and I will
give you the crown of life.'" Revelation 2:8-10 (NIV)*

In trials and sorrow
there is comfort in
someone standing near
and saying "I know".
Empathy, shared suffering;
tender sensitive vibrations
from a heart that cares.

Jesus says:
"There will be suffering".
He suffered.
"There will be persecution".
He was persecuted.
"There will be trials".
He knows all about them.

Jesus' heart is revealed through pain.
How He agonized for our sin!
And all so He could walk our paths
and truly say to us,
"I know. And because I know,
I AM...
all you will ever need."

INTERCESSION

"Wherefore He is able also to save them to the uttermost that come unto God by Him, seeing He ever liveth to make intercession for them." Hebrews 7:25

He pleads for me,
my precious Savior.
As a cloud from the incense altar
laden with spices sweet,
the aroma rises to God's throne
above the mercy seat.
The power is not His persuading speech
but in His presence there.
Not His words, but in His worth.
He is the Word in glorified flesh
eternally positioned to shroud my sins
in the fragrance of
His intercession.

LOST IN WONDER

"Therefore my heart is glad, and my glory rejoiceth; my flesh also shall rest in hope." Psalm 16:9

Wonder.
It happens with the breaking of day.
The light wraps me in hope,
in anticipation, in joy.

The fresh glow alights on familiarity
so recently covered in darkness,
reminding me that God's mantle of love
brings the ordinary into sharper focus,
and for a moment I sense
my place,
my purpose.
There are no words,
merely the quickening of my heart,
lost in the wonder
of surrender.

ADORATION

"Let everything that hath breath praise the LORD."
Psalm 150:6

"I beseech you therefore, brethren, by the mercies of God,
that ye present your bodies a living sacrifice, holy,
acceptable unto God..." Romans 12:1

I bring my gift to You, O King.
The covering does not shimmer,
unadorned by fancy bows or trim.
Its simplicity, though, contains perfume
painfully distilled,
a victory extracted from struggle.
You and I are both aware
I cannot offer You this gift
wrapped any other way
than in my surrendered self.
Raising my hands,
emptied at last of all
but the frankincense of praise,
I adore You,
Christ, my Lord.

Printed in the United States
51377LVS00002B/1-102